To June -

Tho we are no longer "relatives" we have always & will always be friends.

I Love you

Elsie

2010

Y0-ARN-711

Longtime Friends

An Essence of Life Book

Created by

ANN SKELLY

**Andrews McMeel
Publishing**

an Andrews McMeel Universal company

Longtime Friends text copyright © 1999 Andrews McMeel
Publishing. Illustrations copyright © 1999 Ann Skelly.
Under exclusive license from UR1 International.
http://www.ur1.com.au. All rights reserved. Printed in
Singapore. No part of this book may be used or reproduced
in any manner whatsoever without written permission
except in the case of reprints in the context of reviews.
For information write Andrews McMeel Publishing, an
Andrews McMeel Universal company, 4520 Main Street,
Kansas City, Missouri 64111.

Written by Patrick Regan

ISBN: 0-8362-7169-6

Longtime Friends

An Essence of Life Book

Longtime friends
are family that
we choose—
and
they,
in kind,
choose us.

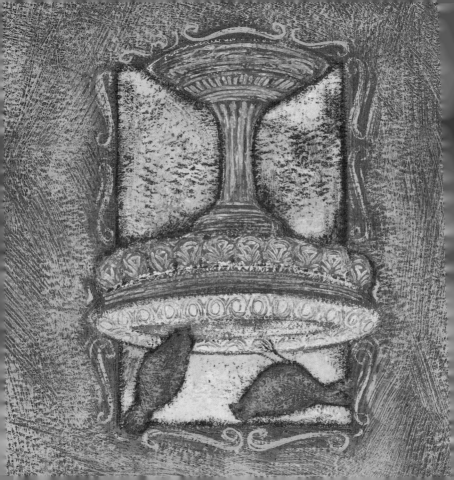

*Such relationships are just as **deep**,*

just as IMPORTANT

as those we are

born into,

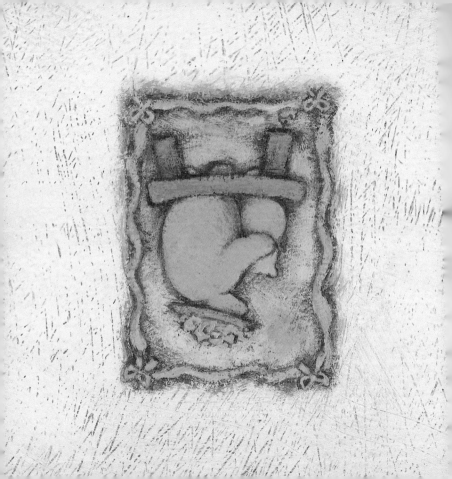

and perhaps more so,

because of the choosing.

We have

chosen

each other.

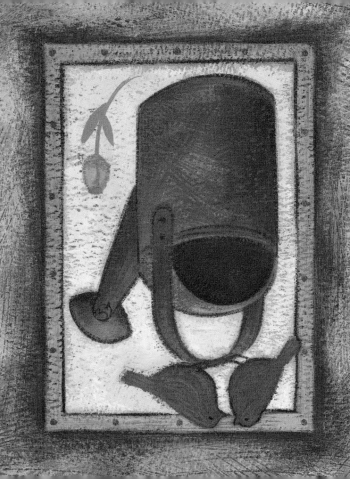

Tempered by the years,
our friendship
has become one of

the treasures

of my

life.

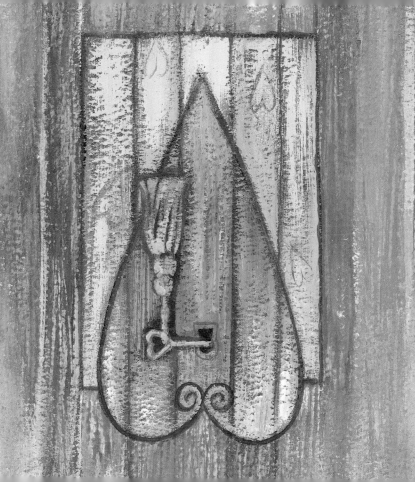

It's depth goes beyond casual shared interests and pleasant conversation.

Let others discuss
the WEATHER outside.
We'll guide each other
through internal *Storms*—
and enjoy the sunshine
together, too.

The difficult times
we've shared have made us
stronger, wiser,
more humble, and
ultimately,
closer to each other.

We ease each other's fears
and share the dreams
too important
to share
with anyone else.

Our
FRIENDSHIP
IS NOT
PRACTICED,
BUT INTUITIVE.

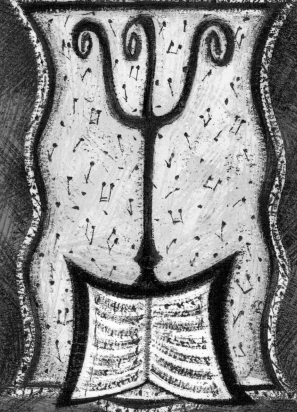

We know when

the other needs

attention, reassurance,

empathy, solitude,

or a gentle push

in the right direction.

Within a well-worn
friendship like ours,
permission
isn't
always
asked,
nor is it required.

And the Grand
gestures of etiquette
are often forgone.

We've grown comfortable

in our friendship,

but as the years

continue to pass,

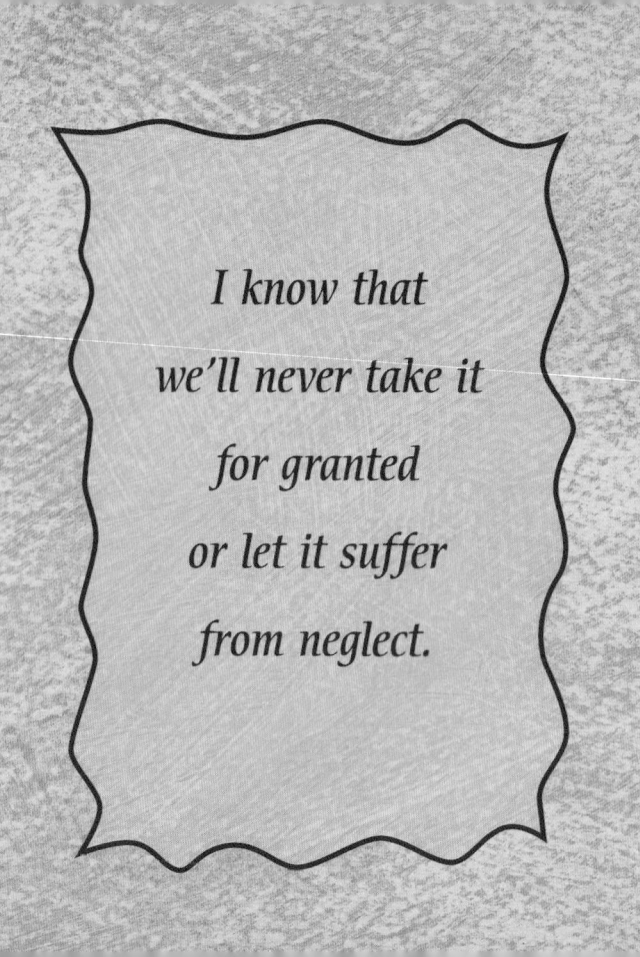

I know that

we'll never take it

for granted

or let it suffer

from neglect.

As we grow older and our lives
grow more complex, it seems
that we have less time for
each other—and the time
we do have always leaves
me wanting more.

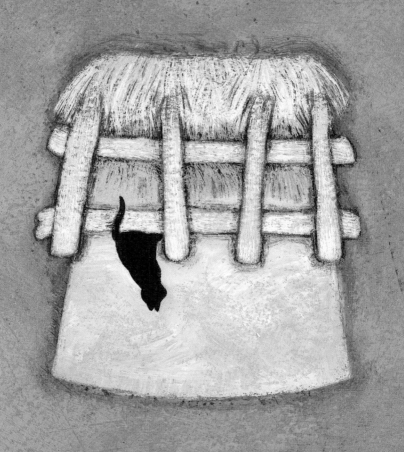

But even during those periods
when we're pulled in

different *directions,*

*our friendship is
just as alive, just as*

RESONANT

to me as when
we are enjoying each
other's company.

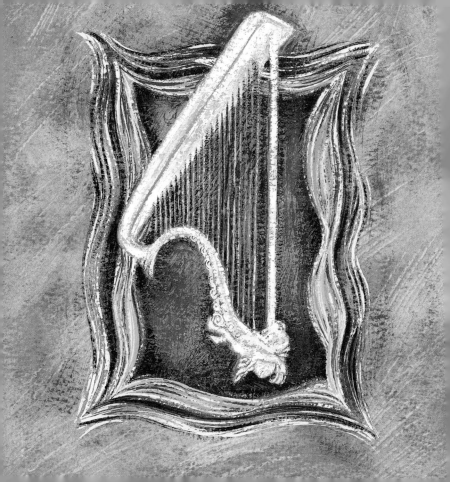

We've taught each other
that when friendship is true,
a hand can be held
from miles away.

We know that
our friendship
will always last
because it
continues to

grow.

and because,
through the years,
we continue to choose
each other.